MARK ANGELO

Illustrated by PATRICIA AND ROBIN DEWITT

One Printers Way
Altona, MB R0G 0B0
Canada

www.friesenpress.com

Copyright © 2023 by Mark Angelo
First Edition — 2023

All rights reserved.

Licensed Use: Major League Baseball trademarks and copyrights are used with permission of Major League Baseball. Visit **MLB.com**

No part of this publication may be reproduced in any form, or by any means, electronic or mechanical, including photocopying, recording, or any information browsing, storage, or retrieval system, without permission in writing from FriesenPress.

ISBN
978-1-03-915384-4 (Hardcover)
978-1-03-915383-7 (Paperback)
978-1-03-915385-1 (eBook)

1. JUVENILE NONFICTION, SPORTS & RECREATION, BASEBALL & SOFTBALL

Distributed to the trade by The Ingram Book Company

DEDICATION

In memory of my brother, Chris,
and the never-ending joy we shared
in going outside to play ball.

★ ★ ★ ★ ★ ★ ★ ★ ★

ACKNOWLEDGEMENTS

A heartfelt thanks to my daughter, Kelly, my wife Kathie, and Jackie Rosser for their valued contributions to this book. Thanks as well to my Dad for the many *Dodgers* games he took me to. He did much to foster and encourage my penchant for the great game of baseball. I also want to acknowledge legendary *Dodgers* broadcaster Vin Scully. I listened to him on the radio each night as a boy and his insightful and lyrically descriptive call of the game made me an even bigger fan!

I was a happy and energetic seven-year-old kid who loved baseball more than anything. The year was 1958, and the *Dodgers* had just moved from Brooklyn, New York to my hometown of Los Angeles.

Dodgers players, both past and present, were my heroes – from the great Jackie Robinson to the home-run king Duke Snider. I wished for nothing more than to be a professional ball player just like them.

I followed the team closely. On nights when the *Dodgers* played, I went to bed early with the radio tuned to the game. I'd usually fall asleep by the fourth or fifth inning, and Mom and Dad would tiptoe in to shut the radio off.

My neighborhood friends were *Dodgers* fans too. There were kids on every corner. While I was the youngest, my older brother Chris and I played with them every day, often only coming home for dinner. Together we'd ride bikes, play catch, and trade baseball cards.

The only thing missing from our neighborhood was a patch of grass big enough for us to play baseball.

But we had a secret. Just around the corner from our house on DeMille Drive, hidden behind a tall hedge with a cave-like opening just big enough to crawl through, was a massive, unfenced lawn. It was a beautiful, seldom-used grassy field that belonged to the great Mr. Cecil B. DeMille, the world's most famous movie director. His house was the biggest I'd ever seen, and to a group of kids longing to play ball, his lawn was calling our names!

So, one hot afternoon in late June, when we were feeling especially courageous, my brother and I, along with our friends, crawled through the secret opening in the hedge to play some baseball.

At first we were nervous about being there, but once we started to play, our anxiety quickly disappeared.

The excitement of playing ball in our very own neighborhood was epic! Hearing the great sounds of the game – like the crack of the bat when you got a hit, the friendly ribbing and chatter between the kids, and the smack of the ball when it hit your glove – made us all feel like we were playing on a real ball field. There was even enough space for my brother to hit his long, towering fly balls, just like Duke Snider!

Mr. DeMille's backyard was just as we thought – the field of our dreams! Even better, no one told us to leave. So we returned the next day, and then the next. Within weeks, the field became a neighborhood gathering spot.

Late that summer though, in the middle of a game, Mr. DeMille's gardener approached us. He said that several of our balls had ended up in Mr. DeMille's prized rose garden.

"You can't play here anymore," he said firmly.

Some of my older friends politely spoke up, claiming there was no other place nearby to play ball. But the gardener stood firm.

"That doesn't matter. There will be no more baseball games."

My friends and I were crushed. We crawled back through the hedge and slowly headed home. Our neighborhood baseball games had abruptly come to an end.

We were a gloomy and discouraged group, yet I felt there had to be something we could do. From what my parents had said, I knew that Mr. DeMille was the greatest "maker of movies" there ever was. And while he lived on our street, he was a man I had only ever seen from a distance, or when he happened to drive by in his large black limousine. I suggested we try talking to the elusive Mr. DeMille himself, but I was met with,

"No way! Mr. DeMille is too famous."

I thought we still had to try, and eventually the other kids agreed. So, we all headed off to Mr. DeMille's house. But when we arrived, my friends, all a bit older than me, had second thoughts. They were nervous about going any farther and wanted to stay behind. They decided to hide along the street and wait until I returned.

I was now completely alone. So, I put on my lucky *Dodgers* hat, mustered all my bravery, and slowly walked up the long, steep stairs to Mr. DeMille's grand front door.

I rang the doorbell.

★★★★★★★★

Within seconds, the massive door opened. Standing there was the very tall butler. In a voice lower than any I'd ever heard, he asked what I wanted.

My mouth suddenly became very dry, and my face turned red. I managed to say, "My name is Mark. I live across the street, and I am here to talk to Mr. DeMille . . . about baseball."

"Mr. DeMille is unavailable," the butler replied.

Refusing to give up, I said, "Sir, we have been playing ball in Mr. DeMille's yard. Maybe we were wrong to do that without permission, but we have no other place that's big enough to play. I was hoping I could speak to Mr. DeMille."

Again, the butler replied, "I am sorry, he is not available."

Sadly, I said, "Okay, thank you," and slowly turned to walk away.

Just then, from behind the butler in the distant hallway, I heard a voice say, "Show the young man in."

I stopped in my tracks! "Follow me," said the butler.

I paused for a moment, my heart thumping in my chest. For the first time, I questioned if I had done the right thing. I took a deep breath . . . and entered the house.

The butler led me through the grand entranceway. The house was big, more like a palace, and its sheer size only added to my jitters. We continued down a hall and into a large room overlooking the field where we had been playing.

Standing by a large leather chair, facing the window, was Mr. DeMille.

"Come here, young man," he said.

Feeling anxious, I cautiously approached him and told him my name. I tried to speak slowly and confidently, but the words just poured out. "Mr. DeMille," I said, "I live across the street, and I love the *Dodgers*. And my friends and I want to play baseball more than anything." I took a deep breath and continued: "We love our neighborhood, but there is no place big enough for us to play ball. That's why we've been using your yard."

With a stern look, Mr. DeMille replied, "Yes, I know."

I gulped but went on. I told him that the gardener said we had to leave and that we couldn't play anymore.

Then, with everything I had left, I finally found the words I had come to say.

"Mr. DeMille, can we play baseball in your yard?"

As soon as I uttered the words, he turned his head to the side and stared out the window at his massive lawn. With a serious look that made me even more nervous, he sat in silence for several seconds. To me, it was an eternity.

Finally, he turned back toward me . . . and then a broad smile crossed his face. With a kind look in his eyes, Mr. DeMille declared, "Mark, go tell your friends they can play ball."

I almost jumped out of my shoes.
I looked at him in amazement and said, "Really? Oh, thank you, Mr. DeMille, thank you!" Then I stumbled back a few steps, repeating "Thank you!" again and again.

The butler escorted me out, said goodbye, and closed the door. I sprinted down the stairs, yelling to my friends who were still hiding along the street, *"Yes! Yes! We can play! He said we can play!"*

My brother and the other kids exchanged high-fives all around. Excitement filled the air. As we headed back to the field, they wanted to know every detail of what Mr. DeMille had said.

When we got back to the hedge, we crawled through the small opening, picked teams . . . and played ball.
Once again, we could pretend to be our *Dodger* idols. To me, it was extra special knowing that Mr. DeMille himself might be watching from his window.

The author in 1958

AUTHOR'S NOTE ✦✦✦✦✦✦✦✦

For the remainder of the summer of 1958, we continued to play baseball on Mr. DeMille's property. Even when the school year started, we still found time to play there.

Sadly, in January of 1959, Mr. DeMille passed away. His family still allowed us to play for the next couple of years until that part of the property was sold and developed into a new home.

Now, in my later years, when I watch my grandchildren play baseball, I'm often transported back to the field of my youth. I'll always remember the grace and generosity of a man who allowed a group of neighborhood children to be just that: children.

Equally as important, those days in the DeMille backyard nurtured what became my own belief that parks, sports fields, and places to play ball should be readily accessible to every child.

ABOUT THE AUTHOR ★★★★★★★★

MARK ANGELO has been a baseball fan since he was a little boy! He is also a globally renowned river conservationist and the founder of World Rivers Day, now celebrated by millions of people in over one hundred countries. Among his many accolades, Mark is a recipient of the Order of Canada, the country's highest honor. His acclaimed debut children's book, *The Little Creek that Could*, is the true story of a stream that came back to life. Through his work with groups such as the Outdoor Recreation Council of BC, Mark has been a long-time advocate for outdoor spaces for all to enjoy. *Can We Play Baseball, Mr. DeMille?*, about a young boy's search for a place to play ball, recounts an actual experience from his childhood. Mark lives in Burnaby, British Columbia, with his wife, Kathie.

CPSIA information can be obtained
at www.ICGtesting.com
Printed in the USA
LVHW010903180623
750103LV00011B/130